# Endorsements

Lisa Ritz is an amazing woman of God whose love for the Lord shines through her very being and pours out to everyone she meets. When she sings, her joy in the Lord is evident and the beauty of her voice reflects the beauty of her Savior. I had the privilege of getting to know Lisa as a student in my high school chorus. What a blessing to see the woman of God she has become! I'm grateful to the Lord for His faithfulness in her life and pray that her willingness to share her journey will be a great encouragement to all who read her story.

~ Soli Deo Gloria - Alone to God Be the Glory
SDG Music Ministry
Dan Meredith

Lisa Ritz's inspired book is a treasure box full of spiritual jewels. Her beautiful book will speak to your heart. You will discover that God calls you altogether lovely and He longs for you to be set free!

~ Betty Lockhart
Nehemiah Ministry

A true leader who has the ability to inspire others isn't born without adversity. As the reader explores Lisa's story, he or she will be able to reflect on their own life struggles and circumstances and become "Beautiful and Free". As you embark on Lisa's journey, you will be able to look at your own life how God sees you in spite of your trials. Never give up hope, and never give up faith! God has plans for you. Read this book!

~ Joel Yount
Spirit Fuel

This book is about the healing God supernaturally poured out on Lisa. God has opened doors for her and she has had the faith to walk thru them. She has truly blossomed and is experiencing a walk with God that has transformed her. She now sees herself just as her Savior sees her ~ Beautiful and Free.

~ Bernice Michael
Founder Breath of God Ministries

I believe God places each one of us on Earth to not only learn but teach others with the gifts we have been given. God has blessed my friend Lisa with many gifts, several of which I have learned from and been blessed by. Lisa has a gentle, loving and infectious spirit! She also has a voice of an angel. I got to experience several of these gifts starting from age 18 when we first met as roommates and friends in nursing school. The next gift came several years later when she sang at my wedding. Now everyone besides myself gets to benefit from her infectious and loving spirit through her life journey thus far.

Beautiful and Free not only will allow you to see Lisa's heart and true spirit but will give you the courage to dig deep in your soul to discover your purpose in life. It will inspire you to become beautiful and free. Thank you, Lisa for sharing so many of your gifts to help each one of us grow in our own journey through life. I love you!

~ Pam Allison Patrick
President
Power2BFit, LLC

The inspiring words written by Lisa will change one's life forever as she discovered, how pain leads to an incredible journey of ultimate gain.  Amazing, Amazing, and yes it is Amazing.

"He Calls me His Lady" is an inspiring quote, I believe will transform the lives of many people.  Lisa's journey helped define what true love really is, and what it should be in a relationship that illuminates the love, intimacy and passion of our Lord and Savior Jesus Christ.

Lisa's intimate walk with Christ, displayed through the love of her grandmother, set the tone of a love she would discover for eternity and that is the Love of Christ, in whom her heart truly does love.  As Lisa found this amazing love, I believe every person that reads this book, will experience what true love really is, when you are truly loved with a Christ like love.

Faithful,

~ Gloria Murray
Women's Ministry
Keepers of the Flame Church

*Beautiful and Free* brings forth a story all too familiar, to so many people; that of being hurt and rejected at a young age. Lisa's transparency will release others to realize God loves them for who they are. Isaiah 61:3 says, "and provide for those who grieve in Zion, to bestow on them a crown of beauty instead of ashes, the oil of joy instead of mourning and a garment of praise instead of a spirit of despair." Lisa's story is one of ashes to beauty, one of restoration and redemption.

~ Ted and Tona Brant
Seeds of Glory Ministries

A love story. Captivating, compelling, heart-stirring, anointed. The descriptive details of Lisa's childhood memories captures your heart. You become engrossed in her words and begin to experience her memories as though they belonged to you. Lisa's love for God and her family is evident throughout her writing.

~ Kathy Ziegler
Women's Ministry
Keepers of the Flame Church

Growing up with Lisa and her family, I have seen Lisa's story come to life. I have seen God's work in her life and her desire to spread His love and message to the nations. Lisa has been an inspiration to her family and friends. Her book will do the same to those who read it. Her story comes from her heart, a heart that is loving and caring. A heart that is *Beautiful and Free.* So if you question who you are in God's eyes, take the journey and see. You will find yourself in this book.

~ Gene Swadley
Friend

I've known this beautiful sister and have had the honor of calling her my friend for over 30 years. She has always carried herself with grace and integrity no matter what is going on around her. This book will bless you more than you can imagine. Lisa's struggles, battles, and countless victories will bless and inspire you. When you read the last page and lay this book down your life will never be the same again. You will be filled with His precious presence and feel His precious grace stronger than ever before. I am so excited to hear from her readers of how, through the Holy Spirit, Lisa has delivered her heart to inspire you and change your life forever.

~ Lisa Koontz
Pleasant Grove Christian Church Worship Leader

Through turmoil and pain, rejection and confusion, "Beautiful and Free" delivers the story of a life devoted to the pursuit of Christ and His perfect love. Lisa's strength and determination to tell her story is a testament to God's mighty hand moving in her life. Allow the Holy Spirit to take you on a journey through the pages of this book as God displays His unending love for a life that, He, has truly made beautiful and free.

~ Eric L. Jones
Musician
MHK Worship Band
(Make Him Known)

Lisa writes with such an honest, open, and transparent heart to deliver this powerful message that many would rather keep in darkness. But now is revealed in the light of Jesus' love to bring hope and healing, love and grace, deliverance and restoration, to all who will read her words! This is a much needed message in the days we live! May the Lord bless you abundantly for your courage to sound the alarm!

~ David Lebo
Author
*Abiding Under The Shadow*

# Beautiful and Free
## A Story of Redeeming Love

By Lisa Ritz

Writing Career Coach Press (a division of Writing Career Coach, 14665 Fike Road, Riga, MI 49276) functions only as book publisher. As such, the ultimate design, content, editorial accuracy, and views expressed or implied in this work are those of the author.



ISBN-10: 193828318X
ISBN-13: 978-1-938283-18-5

Cover designed by Thomas Griffin
Cover photos by Tori Griffin

Photographs on the inside of this book are author's personal collection

Photo on page 109, permission from Brian Lake Ministries

## Dedication

Dearest Lord Jesus,

I dedicate this book to you! You are the lover of my soul! You are my delight!
You saved me! You rescued me! And I give you ALL the GLORY!!!

Where would I be—You only know . . . If I could write with the pen of Heaven and sing with the voice of an Angel it would never be enough to say Thank YOU LORD!!! My heart's deepest prayer is this . . . May the story of my life be worship in YOUR eyes!!!
There will never, ever be another who can love me like YOU!!!

I am My Beloved's and HE is MINE!!!!

I HONOR YOU KING JESUS—

This book belongs to YOU!!!

# Acknowledgements

A heartfelt thank you to each one who has had a part in the writing of this book and the birthing of a ministry.

To my family—I thank God for each one of you! I could not have picked any better myself. To my Mom—Ruth—you are the greatest example of Jesus I know! You love deeply and give freely. I am so glad God gave you to me for my Mom. To my Brother and Sister—Brian Ritz and Kathy Rinard—the best friends in the world! I am honored to know you. You and your families are the greatest treasures of my life. You live honestly and love deeply. Seasons change yet family remains. To my Dad, Leon Ritz, and Grandma Ritz—I will meet you in the morning . . . just inside the eastern gate. You have forever touched my life.

To my Pastors Brian and Pam Lake (Keepers of the Flame International Church)—Thank you for loving me and encouraging me and always believing in me. I am so thankful for you and your family. You have changed my life. Your genuine passion for God and caring for others is a true blessing. So grateful for your words "I believe in you" and "I am proud of you". What a privilege to call Keepers of the Flame International Church my home—and I am honored to know you!!!

Thomas Griffin, Tori Griffin and Joel Yount—thank you from the bottom of my heart for all you have done to bring this project to life! Your creative abilities blow me away. I am honored to call you friends!

Gene Swadley, my lifelong friend—I am so grateful for your listening ear and gentle words. You have been a true and faithful friend and brother. Thank you for your support along the way.

A very big thank you to my publisher Tiffany Colter! I am grateful for your wisdom, encouragement and support as we journeyed this road together! To Audricka Jacob—I appreciate all your labor, laughter and "butterflies". May God abundantly bless you both!!!

To Brian Kenney (Brian Kenney Ministries)—You are my coach, mentor and friend. I bless the day we met. There are not words to say all that I feel. I am so thankful for you. You have listened, encouraged and guided me. You let me cry! You let me roar! And you always believed in me. You taught me to dig deep! And dared me to be Free and Dream Big!!! Fly!!! Bless you my friend!

## Table of Contents

## Foreword by Brian Lake

Beautiful and Free is about breaking through to the new so that your past does not dictate your future. By God's grace, and with the Presence of the Holy Spirit accompanying her, Lisa revisits her past so she can bring us all on a journey of love, of hope, of healing and of faith through the reality of His outrageous love.

Beautiful and Free will minister healing to some of your deepest wounds – the ones that keep you from loving yourself and others. If you have suffered unjustified wrongs that have left a path of destruction and bitter memories, allow Lisa's story to lead you to the love and healing power of Jesus that will free you from the memories and pain of those events. Often those memories keep us shackled to the pain, limiting us from moving into our destiny. Lisa's testimony and profound insights will guide you in becoming a true lover of God so you can move forward in wholeness, rest and strength.

As you read, you'll follow Lisa on her journey as she finds her way through the pain to be released and freed from her past into the compassionate and loving arms of her Savior. She encourages you that no matter what challenges or obstacles are in your life you can trust that God can, through His healing power, bring freedom and turn that pain into a place of blessing and favor that will lead you toward your destiny. You will find yourself falling in love with Jesus!

God's healing love is available to everyone, in every realm of your life, no matter how fragmented you are in body, soul or spirit. His love offers hope and healing to those who trust in Him, mercy for the healing process, restoration from your wounds, double honor for shame and the grace and mercy to forgive your aggressor.

God has a wonderful plan for your life! Believe it and be released, Beautiful and Free one!!

~ Brian Lake
Brian Lake Ministries &
Keepers of the Flame Int'l Church

## Foreword by Brian Kenney

I have had the pleasure of knowing Lisa Ritz personally for the past two years, and I must say that she is a dynamic woman who has a passion to see people transformed into the image that God created them to be in. Lisa not only talks the talk, but she is one that walks the walk. I have served as a life coach to Lisa, and I have personally witnessed how she has worked hard to overcome obstacles and she has transformed her life to become one whom is beautiful and free. In this book, Lisa shares her personal journey about how God saved her and delivered her from the lies of the enemy. She emphasizes that beauty lies in the eyes of the beholder. This book is a valuable resource for all ages, and it is a must have for today's society when media outlets across the globe are highlighting a false image what you should be and what you should look like. Lisa teaches how to become passionate for God and break free from your past mistakes and hurts and overcome the false images that people have made you live up to. I encourage everyone to read this book and allow Lisa to take you by the hand and lead you on the journey to become beautiful and free. I am honored to make this small contribution to this life-changing book. I believe this book is going to be a blessing and life-changing experience to all those around globe that desire to become beautiful and free.

~ Brian Kenney<br>
America's # 1 Dream Builder Coach<br>
& Founder of Brian Kenney Ministries<br>
Lynchburg, VA

## Introduction

***"Your Royal husband delights in your beauty. Honor Him for He is your Lord."***
***~ Psalms 45:11***

You've heard it said that beauty lies in the eyes of the beholder. The question then is—Who is your beholder?

Join me on this journey as I share my story of how God saved me and delivered me. How my "Royal Husband" revealed to me the truth about beauty and freedom. Let me share with you how He taught me that His eyes are my mirror and His thoughts about me are all that matter.

He calls me His Lady! And He is my Beholder! I found the one my heart does love. In Him, I found the love that I had always longed for—was desperate for. In Him, I have complete security and total acceptance.

How about you? Do you see you as God sees you? Do you know your true beauty?

I believe you may find a bit of yourself in the pages that follow. I invite you to come along with me on this journey to be Beautiful and Free. It is my prayer that you will be forever changed by the power of God's love.

Know this—You are wanted! You are precious! You are the love of HIS life!!! He calls you ALTOGETHER LOVELY and HE longs for you to be BEAUTIFUL AND FREE!!!

# Chapter 1

## Annie Get Your Gun

*"Above all else guard your heart for out of it flow the issues of life."*

*~ Proverbs 4:23*

Within the pages of this book is a message of salvation, restoration and healing. The words written tell a story of hope for the heart and healing of the soul. For this is a story of redemption.

Beautiful mountains, running streams, horses, fishing and puppy dogs. That was my great big little world growing up in Fulton County, Pennsylvania. The grass was green, the skies blue, the water pure and the people real.

## *Annie Get Your Gun*

As a little girl we lived in a two story white house on several acres out in the country. The house had a beautiful rounded front porch with a stain glass window in the front door. And how I loved the grey stone patio out back. I can still hear the sound of the screen door slamming when we ran outside to play. Just off to the right was a lovely lilac bush, and my Mom's tulip bed greeted you as you came in the drive. On the other side of the property were a big old cherry tree and a majestic weeping willow. And, of course, I could never forget the old red barn that housed our chickens and a tall chestnut colored horse named Doc. The smell of the hay from the barn and sound of the chickens clucking filled the air. This place made my heart feel happy, safe and free.

Catching lightening bugs, digging for fishing worms, playing with our beagle puppies while running free in the fresh country air—life was good and times were simple back then. I loved my corner of the world and wouldn't trade it for anything.

A happy hearted, bright-eyed girl born to conqueror the Wild West. Even at that young age my heart knew it was the simple things that were the best—and all these years later I still believe that to be true.

My Dad, Leon, delivered fuel oil around the area. Sometimes he would take me along for the day. I always looked forward to going with him and riding in his big red work truck. I was his little helper, and he was my hero. There was one day that was extra special. We drove in that big red Fleming truck for about an hour to a place called Rosco's. There my Dad

surprised me with a sweet beagle dog named Rosie. She was so pretty and gentle. Rosie had puppies, and my sister Kathy and I used to dress them up like doll babies and push them around in our baby buggies. When my Dad saw us he would remind us "Them there are huntin' dogs"—well they were our babies, too. He would just smile and shake his head—I think he kind of thought it was cute.

Saturday evenings were reserved for a family trip to Lanehart's Store to get a coke and a poke of candy. After we got our treats, we would head back down the road to watch *Hee Haw* and *Gunsmoke* on the television. Still makes me smile after all these years. The fond memories of being with my family will always hold a special place in my heart.

Doc was our tall, red, chestnut sorrel horse. He was such a handsome guy! I would watch my Dad brush and saddle him. I remember the time my Mom, Ruth, brushed Doc's teeth. He didn't think much of that. Several years later we sold Doc to a neighbor. It was a sad day for all of us. We loved him and he was a part of our family. One day, as the school bus was taking us home, someone yelled from the back "Hey, there is a horse following us down the road". I turned and looked. Sure enough, it was Doc. He was coming home.

My Mom was Miss Hancock 1964. She was truly a beauty queen. And, of course, I thought she was the most beautiful Mommy of all. She was such a hard worker—still is. She worked in a sewing factory when I was a little girl. She would garden, can and then work in her flower beds—all the while tending to the laundry, the dishes, a husband and children. I

honestly don't know how she did it all. But she never complained, and she was always there to help us in whatever way we needed. To this day she is still like that. I am so grateful that God gave her to me for my mom.

One of my favorite childhood memories was our trip out west. We loaded up our camper on the back of my Dad's truck and headed out on our great adventure. We drove from Pennsylvania to Colorado, Montana, Wyoming and Texas. We saw the Grand Tetons, Yellow Stone Park and the Great Rocky Mountains. That trip sparked something deep in my soul. I wanted to see the world. I wanted to conqueror the Wild West. After all, I could do anything wearing my cowboy hat, cowboy boots, pink shorts and my pistol holster around my hips. *Annie Get Your Gun*! A big-hearted little girl with an even bigger dream. I couldn't wait for all that life would bring.

I thank God for my family, our home and that area that seems to be the land that time forgot. My parents, my brother and my sister are some of the greatest people I have ever known. I couldn't have picked better people if I tried, and I wouldn't trade them for anything—real people, genuine folks with honest hearts. They gave me a solid foundation for the person that I am today. Thank you Lord.

**"When We All Get To Heaven" (Public Domain)**

*When we all get to Heaven*
*What a day of rejoicing that will be*
*When we all see Jesus*
*We'll sing and shout the victory*

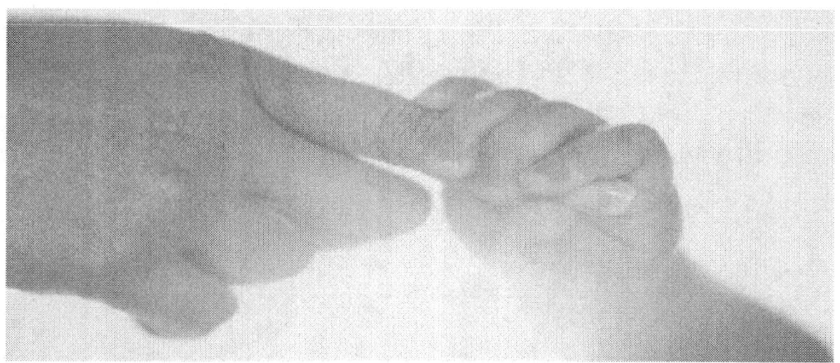

Dear Lord,

Thank you for our dreams. Thank you for a child-like heart and sense of adventure. You placed this in us Lord. For when we are childlike we are closest to our true selves—to the person that you created us to be. Help us God to always dream big for you and for ourselves, too!

Thank you, Father, for the desire to conqueror the Wild West. And thank you, Lord, for our families and those people you have placed in our lives. Truly we are blessed. I ask Father that you bless each heart that would read this book and this prayer. May they find that pure-hearted, childlike dream that is deep inside of them. And, may they dare to dream again.

And, ps.—a note from this little pioneering cowgirl—I say thank you for the lightening bugs, beagle puppies and a horse named Doc. But, most of all, thank you for loving me.

In Jesus' Name I pray.
Amen.

*Annie Get Your Gun*

What is your dream? What is it that you would do if you knew you would succeed? No limits! What is that yearning deep inside of you that makes your heart smile? Your passion is your destiny! Dream Big!

# Chapter 2

## Grandma's Girl

***". . . leave her alone for she has done a beautiful thing".***
***~Mark 14:6***

The very first song I ever remember singing was "Where the Roses Never Fade". My Grandma Ritz sang it with me when I was just 3 years old. To this day I can still feel her presence and hear her voice and see her smile. If love had a name ~ it would be hers—Gladys Leona Ritz. Born August 24, 1920—Home on December 9, 1990. Her legacy—*eternal.*

My Grandma Gladys Leona Ritz was my best friend. I pray somehow God would give me the words to paint a picture of her heart and her love for Jesus and the wealth of wisdom and

joy she would give to me.

"How's my girl?" she'd say with a smile as bright as the sun. She had rosy, red cheeks and the kindest voice. She would give you a hug of pure love. A piece of heaven—especially for me—and I knew I was Grandma's girl.

By earthly measure she didn't have a lot of money, yet she was the wealthiest woman I have ever known. She had all the treasures of heaven in her heart. Her legacy of love has forever touched my life—and that love will change the world.

She lived in a big, old two story house just across the field from my home. It was, without a doubt, my favorite place to visit. When I walked in the door, I was greeted by the sweet smell of wood from the wood stove and then her sweet voice asking "You want a cup of tea?" Her kitchen was so cozy. She had a little twin bed in the corner and wooden rocking chair by the window. We spent many hours in that kitchen. She cooked, she sang and she taught me about Jesus.

I always wanted to spend the night at Grandma's house. It was warm and comfy and full of love. I liked to get her Red Letter King James Bible. I would read every word written in red. Grandma had taught me those were the words of Jesus. Come bedtime, we'd head up stairs. I would ask Grandma to tell me about Heaven. She'd tell me about the gates of pearl, walls of jasper and streets of gold. She'd lean in and say, "But the best part will be when I see Him face to face. What a day that will be."

"Grandma," I'd ask, "Will you pray out loud?" She'd pray with all the fervor of a warrior yet the gentleness of a lamb. One by one, she would pray for her children and grandchildren and call them into the kingdom. In all the years I heard her pray, never once did I hear her ask for anything for herself. She always loved on her Lord and prayed for her family. When I sing the song "There Is a River", I can see her standing there by the River of Life waiting and watching. She is watching for her children and trusting in her Lord to bring them in. I learned the power of prayer in those moments. I also learned the depth of selfless love she had for her family, and I knew I had found a beautiful and powerful place in the presence of God.

One day she told me, "Come with me, Lisa. I want to show you something." We went up the stairs to a little back bedroom. She told me it was something she didn't show everybody, but she wanted me to see it. We walked in and you could feel the presence of the Lord. This was her prayer closet. She explained to me what a prayer closet was. She told me it was the secret place where she came to meet with the Lord. She had a table with a lamp and a ceramic set of praying hands sitting on it. I am so grateful for the depth of what this sweet woman of God lived out before me.

There were many times when I was in the living room that I would hear my Grandma talking in the kitchen. I wondered who she was talking to since it was just the two of us in the house. I went out to the kitchen to see. There she was, hands lifted to heaven, tears streaming down her face and Shekinah glory all over the room. The beautiful brightness of the presence of the Lord was all around her. How she loved her Lord!

On Saturday evenings, she was always so excited to get ready for Sunday morning church. She'd lay out her dress and shoes. She walked across the field to our house and had my Mom roll her hair up in curlers for the next day. Then, the next morning, she'd walk back and get her hair styled . . . all for her Lord. She lived and loved for Jesus.

Many times she taught me about the blood and the body of Christ. It was one of her responsibilities to get things ready for communion. As she prepared the bread, she taught me about the sacrifice of His body and Calvary. Then, as she got the juice ready she'd tell me about the power of His blood. Honestly, I could hardly wait to partake of the bread and the wine. In my childhood understanding, I instinctively knew I wanted and needed His sacrifice. As I write this chapter, I am reminded of how God gave me my very own Bible teacher; how He raised me up.

I loved to go with her wherever she went. They used to call me "Little Gladys". What an honor! She loved to go to revivals. And though she didn't drive, she always found a ride to church. We went to Revival services, and they played the tambourines and people would be singing and shouting. Then, they did the Jericho march. Of course, I thought it was awesome as a six or seven year old child, because I did not have to sit in my seat the entire service. Everyone marched around the church and praised God. I loved it!

One Sunday night when I was about eight it was my Grandma who went forward with me to the altar. My heart pounded as I felt the presence of the Holy Spirit leading me to kneel and receive Jesus as my Savior at that little country church. She was so proud that her girl got saved.

Mays Chapel Christian Church. The church of my childhood. It was the first place I remember seeing the power of God. The place where we would sing "Constantly abiding Jesus is mine . . ." or "When the trumpet of the Lord shall sound and time shall be no more . . . when the roll is called up yonder I'll be there" and ". . . bringing in the sheaves—bringing in the sheaves . . . we shall come rejoicing bringing in the sheaves." I remember I never wanted our services to end. A place of love and kindness and family.

Seasons changed and I grew up. My Grandma was still my best friend. I went away to nursing school a few hours away. I graduated in May of 1988. My Grandma was there with her big smile and even bigger heart. She came to me after the ceremony and began to pray over me. She took my hands in hers and began to speak . . . "These hands, these hands are healing hands. These hands shall touch the sick, and they will recover. These hands shall go to the nations. These hands will go to places that I always wanted to go but never got the chance to go. These hands." At the time, I didn't fully understand the depth of what she was speaking, yet I have never forgotten them. And those words stirred a desire for the nations in my heart. And, as I write this book, I am following that call to the mission field. It is my heart's desire to speak life to those who feel hopeless and forgotten. I pray that God

would use me to heal the sick and the hurting.

December 9th, 1989 Gladys Leona Ritz got to meet her Lord. He was the one she had longed for and the one she had lived for. And, I am convinced she is still hugging on Him. It broke my heart to let her go, yet I could not wish her back. I never imagined my life without her. Her heart, her smile, her words, her song, her prayers, her love. And yet she lives on. She lives on in her children and grandchildren and those who knew and loved her. I am thankful for her legacy of love. These hands will go in Jesus' name to the nations. And as I touch those people with these hands, I know without a doubt that she will be right there with me.

**"Oh How I Love Jesus" (Public Domain)**

*There is a name I love to hear*
*I love to sing its worth*
*It sounds like music in mine ear*
*The sweetest name on earth*
*Oh How I love Jesus*
*Oh How I love Jesus*
*Oh How I love Jesus*
*Because He first loved me.*

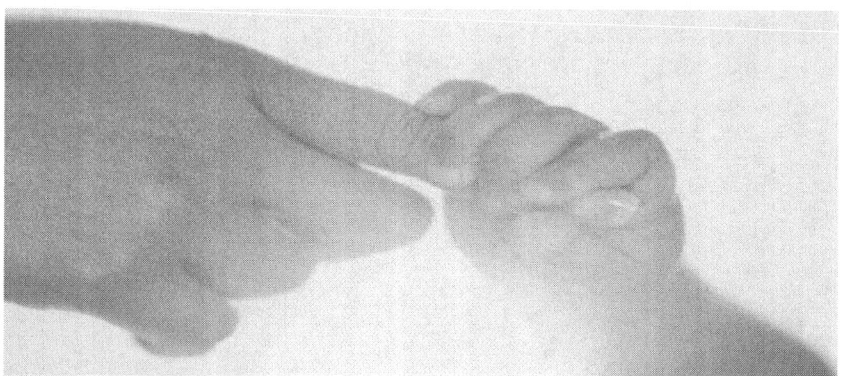

Heavenly Father,

I pray each person who reads this chapter has someone in their life to love them like my Grandma loved me. That they would know unconditional love. Lord, may they feel the sweetness of Jesus and know the comfort of His touch.

And, Lord, if they don't have someone like that I ask that you bring that person into their lives right now in Jesus' name. I also ask, Lord, that you help each one of us to be that person. To reach out in love and teach and speak and serve—for you, Lord.

Thank you, Lord, for my Grandma. I am undone when I think of her and how she loved You—how she loved me. How she lived her faith. I am forever grateful. And now, Lord, all that was poured in, may it be poured out.

In Jesus' Name I pray.
Amen.

*Grandma's Girl*

If love had a name, whose would it be? Who is the person that touched your life in a powerful way? What were those things they did to make a difference?

What are some of the ways that you could reach out to others?

Lisa

My childhood home (the early years)

Mom and Me

Dad and Me

Me and my saddle...Ready to go!

Dad and Me

Mom, my sister, Kathy,
and Me. Our trip out West

Dad, my sister, Kathy,
and Me. Our trip out West

My Grandma Ritz

Dad, Mom, my sister,
Kathy and Me. Easter

# Chapter 3

## What Happened to My Life

***"Unto Thee, Oh Lord, do I lift up my soul."***
***~ Psalms 25:1***

Last night I was at the grocery store getting my groceries for the week. I felt good about myself. My cart was filled with fresh fruits and vegetables and other organic foods. The woman scanned my purchases, and I counted out the money.

"Mommy, why is she so big like that?"

It was an honest question from a child yet one that still pierces my soul to the core. In a flash, all the positive feelings I had felt vanished. My heart ached with shame, rejection, fear and pain. The ghosts of insults past echoed inside of me, and suddenly a once healthy grocery cart seemed like my enemy.

What hurt even more was that her question was an honest one and, quite frankly, a question I had asked myself many, many times. “Why am I so big like this?”

I went to my car and drove home in tears. I was angry. It wasn’t fair.

I made it to my home where I sat on my sofa and decided to eat a bag of Doritos and drink a Pepsi. Forget the spinach and kale! Forget the fresh fruit! Forget it all! I was undone! And the battle for my soul was on!!!

This is not an easy chapter to write. Yet, even as I write it there is healing. What is hidden cannot heal. Transparency brings healing.

As you read, rest assured this is not the end of the story. There is a rescue. There is a hero! And there is restoration and redemption! But for a few moments, walk through this part of the story with me. Who knows, as you walk it you may find your own freedom!!!

Maybe you’ve asked the same questions I have: “Why Me?” “Why did this have to happen to me?” “Why Lord?” Questions I would ask myself day after day as a small child. The wonder of my early years had been stolen, and I was held captive in a sad, dark, lonely world. What happened to my life?

I was no longer Little Annie, Daddy's little sweet thing or Grandma's girl. Starting in kindergarten, and continuing through high school, my names were Fatty, Fatty Two-by-Four, Hefty, Tub of Lard, etc. I was five years old the first time I heard someone say something awful like that to me. When you are that young, you just absorb what is said. Soon you believe it. Maybe the names you heard didn't have to do with weight. Maybe you were called short, ugly, dumb or nerd. Those names begin to write their message on your heart. Gone were the days of "Annie Get Your Gun" and my little word of lightening bugs, puppy dogs and fishing worms. The battle for my soul, my destiny and my dreams had begun.

I remember the deep, deep pain of being laughed at and made fun of. I dreaded each morning, knowing I would have to get on the school bus. Someone would snicker as I walked by or shout out a humiliating word. I would walk and act like I didn't hear it. But I heard it. In fact, I heard it in my soul. No child—or, for that matter, no living being—should ever have to endure such pain, shame and rejection. Even now when I look at my picture as "Annie"—the little cowgirl—versus my kindergarten picture, I can see the sadness of my heart. And once again I would ask, "What Happened to my Life?"

My life at home in those years was very painful as well. My parents are wonderful people, and I love them dearly, but they did not see I was dying on the inside. I felt as if I lived in my own world. I knew they loved me, yet because of the trauma in life I could not feel their love.

The years of low self-esteem, low confidence and self-

consciousness were overwhelming. I lived in deep fear—every moment of my life—of being laughed at, shamed or humiliated because of my weight. Couldn't they see I was a person? A good person? With a heart and feelings? Sometimes it felt as if I was inhuman—some type of a monster or something.

Because of my size, I was never able to wear clothes the other kids wore. Most of my clothes were sewn by my Mom or a friend. Even when we had parties at school, I had to make a homemade costume because none of the store bought costumes ever fit me. So many little things like these others may take for granted. Later stores started to make fashionable clothing in larger sizes, but the shame of those years, the pain of feeling so different still burned in me. I believed the lies that danced in my brain. No man would ever want me. Or, who would ever date me? The attack of the enemy was severe.

It was when I was about six or seven that the unthinkable happened. I was molested. Another blow of the enemy. Innocence lost. Devastation, rejection, self-loathing and even greater shame entered. No need to share the details and no good would come in sharing the names. All is forgiven. If you've suffered this same painful encounter, then you know the very deep painful downward spiral it brings. Not only did I have to bear the pain of looking different, now I was "ruined" for sure and would bear the shame of molestation.

As a little child, I didn't fully understand the depth of all that happened in those years. For me, in my childlike mind, the world I once knew and cherished was forever gone. Even at

that young age, I felt that my life was gone. It is a horrible place to be, but in my mind I had decided I would pick myself up by the bootstraps and create the best life I could with what had been dealt to me.

It was such a difficult time. I decided if I could learn to quickly engage in conversation and be extra nice to people then maybe they wouldn't be so quick to laugh at me. I became very good at engaging people. I also opened myself up at the heart level, thinking if they see I am good person then they won't reject me. Unfortunately, the plan I'd created to protect myself only brought more pain. These two decisions would later cause me unbearable heartache. I would open my heart to people only to have them reject me. I also already believed at the age of ten that no man would ever be attracted to me or ever want to date me. I decided I would just settle for being friends with guys and play the matchmaker for all of my friends. Yet deep in my heart I longed to be loved. I longed for someone to think I was beautiful.

My weight had already become a focal point in my life. I was put on my first diet at the age of 10. My doctor told me that blood tests showed that my thyroid was not functioning properly. You might think that would relieve me, that there was a fix, but it actually made me sad. Another thing wrong with me. Now nobody would ever, *ever* want me. I would diet and lose the weight then gain the weight. All the while I lived in self-hatred.

In junior high, I decided to take matters into my own hands. I decided to starve myself. I was determined to do whatever it

took to be thin. For a month I drank one gallon of water per day and ate either one dill pickle or one slice of Lebanon bologna. I lost 40 lbs in a month. Awesome, right? Not! Every morning, I passed out in the shower. Every time we had gym class I would see stars. But, hey, I lost the weight. The recognition from everyone else was all the positive reinforcement I needed.

After a while, I couldn't take passing out any more, so I began to eat again. I ate what the rest of my family ate, yet I started to gain back the weight. I had worked too hard and suffered too much to let that happen, so I decided I would make myself throw up to keep the weight off. Had no idea it was called bulimia and that it was considered an eating disorder—and that I could be placed on the psych ward for help. I only knew it was a way I could eat like everyone else and keep my weight off. Losing weight had given me the positive notice and approval I'd craved since that first awful day in kindergarten. I would do what I had to in order to keep that approval.

Then, months later, I began to notice a difference in my voice. All the vomiting was hurting my vocal chords. For me, the one thing I had was my song. And weight or no weight, I was not willing to sacrifice the song of my heart—my love for Jesus. Honestly, this was the only reason I stopped. I was not going to let this take my song!

All the pain of being overweight and laughed at, being molested and having an eating disorder was more than I could take. Depression had overwhelmed me. I felt such a deep, deep sadness, and I had come to the end of trying to live this

nightmare. Things got so bad that in senior high I had decided to end my life. After all, no guy would ever want me, my body was ugly and the pain of the shame and humiliation was more than enough. I decided I was going to drive my vehicle down Black Oak Road. There was a row of oak trees there. If I drove my car down that road at 90 miles an hour and drove into those trees it would be over. I thought if the first tree didn't get me the next one would. But God intervened. I just couldn't go through with it, and the songs of my early years—the words and prayers of my Grandma—covered me. And in that moment I believed ever so lightly that maybe it could get better.

I really don't think anyone realized the pain I lived in. I was very good at putting a smile on my face and acting as if all was well. I smiled when I wanted to frown. I laughed when I really wanted to cry, and I pretended everything was fine.

The years went by. Times changed but the haunting continued. I learned to believe all those lies as the truth. I had been in several dating relationships that just never worked out. I still couldn't wear "normal" clothes, nor could I do many things I longed to do. But I still had my Lord and my song. And, at just the right time, God stepped in and began to unravel my crazy, crazy world. He began to set the crooked places straight. He replaced the lies of the world with the truth of His Word. He began to show me—the real me!

In the next chapter, I will share some of that journey—this journey. Not an easy path, as you will see. But I have learned that only God knows the journey of the soul. And only God can bring you out. I have learned He is faithful and what He says He will do. He shows me every day it's who He says I am that is the truth--and that is all that matters. I have come to believe "All Thy works are wonderful" . . . and that includes me.

**"Jesus Love Me There" (Lisa Ritz. Copyright 2013)**

*In the sad and lonely places/in the dark and empty spaces/in that place where no one else can see*
*– Jesus, only you*
*– only me*
*– Jesus love me there.*

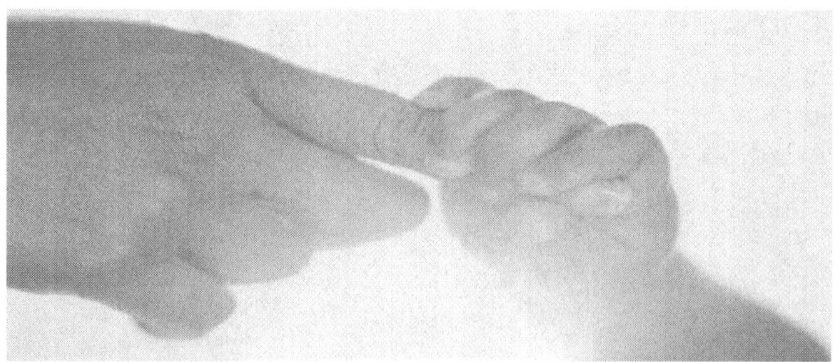

Heavenly Father,

In my natural mind, I will never understand the reason for all the pain. There isn't a bucket big enough for all the tears. Yet, I put my trust in You. You have never forgotten me nor abandoned me. And You have proven yourself to be faithful and true.

It is my prayer for each one that reads this chapter to see it with the eyes of their heart. May they know they are not alone. May they be mindful of the power of their words. May they have the strength to surrender to the power of Your love. For truly it is Your Love that heals and sets free. You make all things beautiful in Your time.

In Jesus' Name I pray.
Amen.

Is there some hidden place of your heart that you want God to heal? You don't have to write it here—HE will see it. Truth is, HE already does. Somehow there is freedom that comes when we let it out. So, if you choose to, I encourage you to write the hurt, the pain, the loss on these next few pages. What is hidden cannot heal. It's not what we do—it is what we surrender. Will you surrender the pain?

# Chapter Four

# Will You Marry Me

***"I have found the one my soul doeth love."***
***~ Song of Solomon 3:4***

You have heard it said "Beauty lies in the eyes of the Beholder". The question, then, is "Who is YOUR beholder?"

For so many years of my life I lived in sorrow and pain and fear. I barely remembered that little cowgirl who wanted to conqueror the Wild West. The innocent, uninhibited dreams of my childhood were forever gone—and what would happen to Grandma's Girl? Do you have dreams you've given up as life has beaten you down? It seems as we get older our dreams become smaller.

I would ask the Lord many, many times: Why? Why? Why? Why? Why did this have to be my life? Why did those things have to happen to me? So many questions, and in my mind I had set my path to make the best life I could with what had been dealt to me. My innocence was stolen and the pain of shame and rejection was more than anyone should have to bear. The sound of the names I heard day after day began to take its toll on my heart. The pain shifted to anger inside of me. It wasn't fair that people treated me as they did.

The anger turned to depression. Each day I would wake up with such sadness in my heart. It seemed I lived in some type of a dark heavy cloud. I felt all alone and lost in the world. The cycle of weight gain and weight loss was repeated many times in my life. I wondered why I had to eat differently than everyone else. How could I live in the same house, eat the same food as the rest of my family—and yet I was the only one who had issues with being overweight. The struggle with weight and body image that began in early childhood would continue into my adult life.

I was so very desperate to be loved. I just wanted someone to think I was beautiful. Somebody. Anybody. You know what I mean, ladies, we want to know things like "Do you see me?" "Do you think I'm pretty?" I lived in a faraway place in my heart. I felt so different and disconnected from the rest of the world. The pain of loneliness was almost unbearable at times. I continued to be happy for those around me, but in my quiet times I felt hollow inside. There was a deep rooted emptiness that was hard to explain and that gnawed at me, taking away more and more of the true parts of me.

I struggled to find my way. I knew the Lord. I went to church. I read my Bible, and I prayed. Yet something was missing. I tried to create that missing piece for myself for many years. I would try to make myself look pretty by using makeup or having "perfect" hair. I made sure I did all the "right" things. I treated people kindly, worked hard, had a nice home, etc. But no matter what I did, I continued to have a deep longing on the inside of me that needed and wanted to be free.

I settled for relationships that were a set up for rejection and a repeat of the cycles I had lived so many times. Some of the relationships were one-sided and some of them were verbally abusive. I would be drawn to men who did not honor me. I would lay my heart wide open only to have it stomped on and kicked aside. It would leave me feeling unworthy and broken wondering what was wrong with me.

I recall a relationship I had years ago when I thought I had found the man of my dreams. He was tall, dark and handsome. Very cultured and educated and extremely charming. We started as neighbors and then became "friends". Several months into the friendship we became a couple. I don't even know how it happened. One thing led to another, and I found myself in a relationship with someone I really didn't know. He professed to believe in God and even said he believed in Jesus, but simply believing in something doesn't mean you are saved. I pray that one statement alone will save someone from going through a lot of pain.

My seeming prince charming knew how to charm me. We went out to nice dinners and to the movies. We spent evenings

shopping and weekends going to international festivals. I thought he was “it”. Unfortunately, as the warning signs came I chose to ignore them. He never professed that he accepted Jesus as his personal savior. He attended church with me a few times and went to some singles activities but something was off—and I knew it. In my desperation to be loved, I explained each and every warning away. My desperation to be loved and to have someone think I was beautiful overshadowed the nudging of truth I felt in my spirit.

After the initial warnings, the problems became more visible and intense. He disapproved of the way I pronounced certain words. I was not allowed to buy clothes from certain places. He would quiz me daily on what I ate and how long I exercised. This only fed in to my obsession over my weight and appearance, and I didn’t need his help. I was obsessed at that point about what I ate. I spent three to four hours per day working out! EXTREME!!!

Then, one night when we were together I noticed he was touching my arm and then my leg. At first I thought he was just being nicely affectionate. It felt good to be touched, appreciated and loved. I pushed away the other thoughts. Then, I realized he was measuring me! Yes! Really! Measuring me! And the awful part is, I stuck around. I tolerated it. I did not believe better of myself. I was willing to be treated like that out of my desperation to be loved and my lifelong desire to be married.

Finally, several months later the relationship ended. He admitted he was not a Christian. I was heartbroken and devastated, yet deep within I knew God had protected me. I wasn't willing to end it because of how he treated me, but I was not willing to go in to a relationship where Christ wasn't the center.

A few years later, I found myself at the opposite end of the extreme. I was going to make sure I had me a good solid Christian man! Right? Am I right?

I met a nice young fellow at my church who was going to Bible College to be a preacher. I watched him for several months. I was determined to never get into the same situation I had just come out of.

This soon-to-be preacher man and I began to date. I think that's what you call it. We had to make appointments to talk with each other on the phone because he was busy with the Lord's work and didn't have time for me. And, once again, I tolerated it thinking, "Well, he is a preacher man taking care of God's business?"

After several months of "phone dates" and a few face to face evenings, He proposed to me. Hallelujah! Thank you Jesus! He asked me to marry him!

Bliss. Bliss. Finally, I had found a man of God who wanted me to be his Mrs. The only problem was, he never did honor me or our relationship. He constantly cancelled dates, frequently forgot to call and put almost everything and

everyone else before us. One evening on the phone I confronted his behavior. He became quite angry and rebuked me! Yes. Rebuked me.

Finally, I saw the light and had enough. I ended the engagement and mailed the ring back to him. What a time! Looking back, I can't believe the things I did out of desperation to be loved and wanted and the need to feel "beautiful". Have you ever found yourself in this type of relationship? If so, dear one, keep reading—there is hope and there is healing for you.

I repeated this pattern a few more times until the Lord confronted me.

There was a Bible study on marriage at my church. I had read books and listened to programs, etc. Now I was going to hear what God had to say about marriage. I felt like I was on the altar of God. Some things in my life and thoughts in my mind had to die. God showed me that my desire to be married was an idol in my life. The dying process was painful and there were many times I wanted to crawl off the altar, but I knew I must stay there until that idol was dead. I would go before the Lord with my desire for a mate and beg to know why I was still single. The Lord revealed to me during my prayer time that I desired a mate more than I desired God. I knew it was the truth. I had to realign the desires of my heart and release it to God. God had brought me to the place of total surrender. And it was at that time that HE began to show me HE was my HUSBAND and I was his BELOVED. He spoke His words to

my heart. I felt the sweetness of His presence, and I knew He cared for me.

I have learned that no one will ever love me the way JESUS can!!! Jesus found me in my sad and lonely desperation. He came so far for me! He began to show me how HE saw me. He began to heal the deep, deep wounds of my soul as HE unlocked the places I had hidden. Secret places. Secret wounds. There were many things there I didn't want to face. Some of them were things people had done to me. There were other things that I had done wrong. I had to accept my part in them. All of these things I'd hid from others and from me, yet they were not a secret to HIM. And no matter how bad or how awful I thought those things were, HE LOVED ME!

He came to me. He rescued me. He wooed me with HIS presence. He showered me with HIS extravagant LOVE!!! He reached down into the deepest part of my wounded broken hurting soul and totally healed my heart! Ah, Lord Jesus! You are my Royal Husband! In that time He revealed to me that I am HIS LADY! He will never leave me. He always honors me, and HE treats me with tenderness and gentleness. His love is deeper and wider and higher than my heart can contain. I had been romanced by the King, and I would never, ever be the same. I have found the One my soul does love. I am my Beloved's and HE is mine. TRUE LOVE.

The love of God expressed to us by Jesus, His Son and revealed to us through His Holy Spirit.

"For God so Loved"; "God so Loved"; "God so Loved"!!!! (John 3:16) HE loves you!!! He is jealous for you. He is passionate about you. He calls you altogether lovely. He is the hound of Heaven who is pursuing you even as you read these words. I pray right now, in the name of Jesus that if you do not know Jesus as your personal savior; if you have never asked Him to forgive you of your sins and to come into your life — then let this be that moment. I promise you HE will meet you right where you are. There is no place you have been that would keep Him from loving you. There is nothing you have done that would make Him turn away. HE LOVES YOU!!! OH, HOW HE LOVES YOU!!!

**"Not Forgotten" (Lisa Ritz. Copyright 2013)**

*He knows your name.*
*He sees your heart.*
*He knows your fears.*
*And you~ you're not forgotten.*
*He's coming for you.*
*Oh you~ you are not forgotten.*

**The Midnight Cry/ My Salvation Story**

As a young girl I went to the altar and gave my life to the Lord. Yet in my teenage years I drifted away from the Lover of my soul. I was not living a life dedicated to the Lord. Well,

one night I was awakened by the sound of a trumpet! A very loud trumpet blasting!!! I awakened in a panic! Oh my goodness—this is it! The trumpet of the Lord shall sound and time shall be no more.... I missed it! I missed Jesus! I was left behind! My heart sank! Now what will I do? I guess I will be one of those who get their head chopped off? Why, oh why, didn't I yield to the warnings of the LORD? Was it worth it? The wrong I had done? The things I thought would bring me joy? Was it worth eternity?

I remember blinking my eyes but I didn't go anywhere. I kept looking up into the night sky and couldn't see anything; all the while, the trumpet was still sounding.

I ran through my house. I checked my parents' bedroom—still there. I ran to my sister's bedroom—she was still there. I was confused. Surely we all didn't miss the rapture. I went back to my bedroom and looked into the sky one last time. Suddenly the trumpet stopped. And immediately I heard the voice of the Lord say –"The next time the trumpet won't wait." Right then and there I fell to my knees. I repented from the depth of my being for the wrong I had been doing. I gave my life to the LORD—every part of me for HIS will and HIS way.

I honestly thought I had missed Heaven. I knew the LORD was warning me. Only the sound of HIS trumpet . . . the time is very short . . . Jesus is coming soon!!! Will you be ready dear one! Make this the moment you respond to HIS love! Say "Yes" to Jesus!

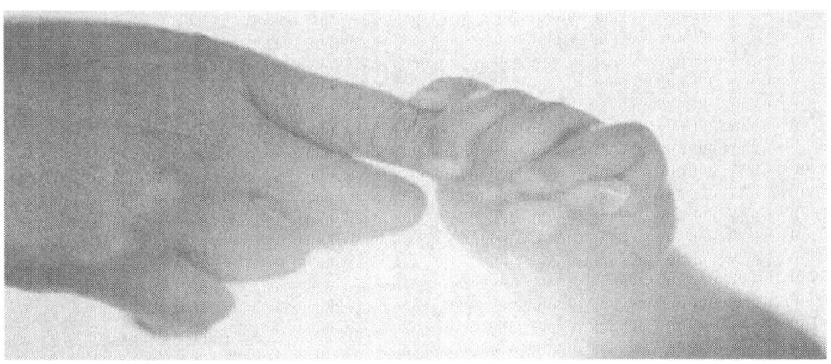

**The Prayer**

Ask Him….Ask Him… He makes it so easy for us. Jesus paid it all. All you need to do is say, "Lord, I admit I have sinned. I am a sinner. I need a savior. Jesus I believe you are the Son of God. I believe you died on the cross for my sins. You didn't just cover them JESUS, your BLOOD took them away. I ask you right now Jesus to come into my life. Come into my heart. Jesus, I need you, and I want you. Be my LORD."

If you said those words and meant them, you are born again! You are going to live with HIM forever and ever! Eternal life! You belong to HIM…. And He belongs to you. It is my prayer that you know HIM more and more. He will reveal himself to you daily. Today you have been born again . . . you have a new life in Christ… you are a brand new creation.

Beloved….Be - Loved!!! Dear one, Heaven is celebrating you!!!

What have you done out of desperation to be loved?

***HE knows. HE sees. HE cares.***

Ask HIM to show you how much HE loves you. Write what HE speaks to your heart.

## Chapter Five

## The Power of Love

***"And the greatest of these is love."***
***~ 1 Corinthians 13:13***

Only God knows the journey of the soul. And only God knows exactly how to heal and speak life to those places. When you look over your walk with God you will start to see those little God kisses—if you care to look for them. The following is a list of some of the encounters I had with the Power of the Love of God. The words tell of the people, places, moments—and yes, even animals—that God used to speak to my broken heart and release the fragrance of His healing.

**Miss America**

2004 was a year the LORD began to teach me about the spirit of rejection. While I had known great rejection and shame in my life, I never really studied the spirit of rejection. It was a layer by layer teaching and healing. Some of those layers hurt when they came off. Yet only GOD knows how much "oomph" and how much love we need in each step along the way. There were times I literally felt like I was going to die. There were so many days I just wished Jesus would come and take me home. The tears I cried and the dark loneliness of the soul were overwhelming at times. I was tired of living in a world where I felt like I did not belong. I always tell people that only God knows the journey of the soul and only God knows how to heal and lead us into freedom.

It was "Question and Answer" evening at the church I was attending at the time. The subject of marriage came up. The teaching turned toward a discussion talking about deposits and withdrawals in marriages. I sat there and wondered what it even had to do with me. I wanted to be married, but I wasn't, and it didn't seem I ever would be. The service was coming to a close when the pastor began to minister. He opened the altar for folks to come and pray. He said "Singles, this is for you, too." He continued, "Some of you have sat there and said—what does this have to do with me? This has EVERYTHING to do with you. This night is for YOU. This night is a set up for YOU." He said, "Some of you have put walls up around your heart and have said NEVER AGAIN. But those walls are keeping the blessing out." In my heart I did not want to go. I did not want to hear one more prayer about being single or

waiting for a mate. My heart was racing inside, and I felt as if it was going to pound out of my chest. I knew God was dealing with me. I knew God wanted to speak to me. In that moment, out of pure obedience, I got up out of my seat and went to the front of the church.

As I stood at the altar, I could see the Pastor walking towards me. I felt the fire of God on him from 20 feet away. He was headed for me and something big was about to happen. As the Pastor walked towards me, I could feel the POWER of GOD all over him. It felt like a wall of fire was all around him. He said "This whole night was for you. This whole thing was about you. God set you up. GOD says, 'I am your husband. I have betrothed you to myself. You belong to me.'" Then with all the authority of heaven the Pastor commanded, "Spirit of rejection LOOSE her!!!"

I tell you, I felt that thing come off me. It felt like a tight rope unwinding off a spin top. That spirit came off of me. In that moment the LOVE of GOD was so thick you could cut it in the atmosphere. God made me feel like Miss America!!! I never felt so much love and acceptance until that moment. FOREVER changed by the LOVE of GOD.

**The Encounter**

It was during our worship service one Sunday morning at Keepers of the Flame International Church. The presence of the LORD was so thick. The aroma of HIS love permeated the

room. It smelled like the fragrance of a sweet rose. As I worshipped I could sense a tangible presence of God. I could feel the weightiness of His presence. I could see the brightness of HIS glory all over the front of the room.

It had been a long, tiring journey to get to this place. There were many disappointments. I had many questions as to whether I heard the voice of the Lord and His call on my life. I was very weary. I had been waiting for something, and I had waited a long time. Have you ever felt like that? You are sure you heard the heart of God for your life, but the wait was so long you had given up? That morning in the presence of the Lord I felt a realignment of the last ten years. I wept as I felt the power of God envelope me. It was as if the Lord had taken me in His arms and wiped away years of tears and doubts. In that moment, I could feel God's arms of love wrap around me. It was a safe place. I knew I had made it, and I knew my heart was home.

What an amazing set up from God that day. Near the end of the service, the Lord spoke to me again. A minister began to speak to me. He confirmed everything God had placed in my heart over the past ten years—things I thought nobody saw. He said God had a song for me. It's not even a Christian song, but this is what the Lord would sing over me today. He began to sing the song to me about how God saw me. God thought I was beautiful. I was everything that God had longed for. I melted in the presence of my KING. God had sung that song to me many times in our private moments. Yet for HIM to sing that to me in front of a group of people was deeply healing to my soul. It was as if all the times I had been laughed at and

made fun of were wiped away in one note and all that mattered was HIS heart for me.

I dropped to the floor weeping in HIS presence. Truly, one moment in HIS presence changes everything.

**Honor—Pastor Brian Lake**

Honor. What does that word mean? What does it look like? For me—the world I knew—I had no clue what honor meant. I had never known honor. The years of being laughed at and made fun of, mocked and humiliated had spoken anything but honor to me. I went to the dictionary to see what the word "honor" meant. Some of the words I found to describe honor were "to show respect"; "to esteem"; "to show admiration". Wow—I had rarely found any of those in my life. UNTIL GOD—

One evening during a service at Keepers of the Flame Church our Pastor had an altar call. I went to the front for prayer. When Pastor Brian came to me to pray—He looked me in the eyes and he said, "Lisa, I want you to know it is an honor for me to know you. I am honored to know you." I began to cry. Those were such powerful words—no one had ever said that to me before. He then got on his knees, and he said, "I honor you Lisa." He said, "I would wash your feet. I am honored to know you. It is an honor for me to know you." I will never forget that moment. There was such a healing that flowed over my heart and soul. It seemed to wash away all the hurtful words, the pain of feeling invisible and the despair of feeling

unseen to the world around me.

I will carry that moment into eternity. I have come to know the power of honor. It is life changing and I am forever grateful. And Pastor Brian—I honor you!!!

**Family**

As I close this chapter on the power of love, I want to thank the Lord for the beautiful gift of my family. I have introduced them to you throughout the lines of this book, and I think it very fitting to share the power of love in our lives.

My Dad and Mom are two of the greatest people I have ever had the privilege of knowing. I could not have picked better parents if I tried. I can see the how the hand of God lovingly chose them for me. My Dad, Edward Leon Ritz was a great man of honor. A man true to his word. His yes meant yes and his no meant no. You always knew where he stood. He was genuine. He never changed in response to his surroundings—whether he was in the woods of Fulton County or in the city of Charleston, South Carolina—he was Dad! I love him for that. He taught me by example. He lived an honest life loving the pure and simple things. I realize now how much wisdom there is in that. He embraced each moment of every day. He loved hunting and fishing and sitting on the front porch. He loved to watch for deer and listen for turkeys. I have so many fond memories of him. I carry his sense of adventure in my heart. He was fearless and proud to be who he was. He never tried to be anybody else—never wanted to be anybody else. I was and

will always be Daddy's little sweet thing. I love and miss you Dad. I will meet you in the morning just inside the eastern gate . . . until then my heart will go on singing!

My Mom, Ruth Marie (Shives) Ritz—Miss Hancock 1964. My Mom is one of the greatest examples of the Lord I have ever met. She is beautiful and kind and always thinking of others. I watch her live out her life in true humility and service to others. She is a missionary every day. She goes out of her way to help others. It may be taking someone to the doctor, baking a pie or cleaning their house or just stopping by for a visit. She is so kind and loving to everyone. As a little girl, I knew I had the prettiest Mommy of all. She worked endlessly with never a murmur or complaint. She never demanded or asked for anything in return. God truly blessed me with the best Mom ever. I have learned so much from her. Her faithfulness and dedication to her family is easily seen by all. Even as I write this, I am reminded of how she is always thinking of others. It may be in cooking us our favorite dinner for our birthday or carefully choosing and wrapping our Christmas presents. I honestly don't think I have ever heard her ask for anything for herself. Growing up I loved to watch her work in her flower beds. There were tulips and irises. She gardened and canned, cooked and cleaned—all with love! I am blessed beyond measure. I love you Mom! You are a beautiful example of all that a Godly woman should be.

The Lord also gave me the gifts of the greatest brother and sister in the world. My sister Kathy and brother Brian are some of the most genuine people I have ever known. I have fond memories of our growing up years. We rode our bikes,

camped in the front yard, went fishing and, of course, we all love Christmas!!! There are so many stories I could tell you, but it's much better if we all sit around the kitchen table or on the carport at my Mom's house and share the memories. My sister is kind and sincere, tender and strong. I am proud to call her my sister and friend. Your fearless singing inspired me to sing and to "Be a Missionary Everyday". You are one of the strongest and loving women I know. My brother is one of the greatest men I know. He is a true friend and a great family man . . . so much like my Dad. He loves hunting and fishing and spending time with his family. Brian, you were sunshine to my world in all those early years. I could always count on your love, hugs and smile. My siblings' children are a blessing to me . . . No matter how old they are I will always be their Auntie . . . God has special plans for them. I love you Adrienne, Garrett, Levi and Tanner Bug!!!

**Puppy Love—My Basil Girl**

And as I close, I must share the love of the most beautiful dog I have ever known. My Basil girl! How I miss her. She was the prettiest cinnamon red chow I have ever seen. Her eyes were kind and her spirit so sweet . . . so sweet. She was a rescue. I found her at the local shelter several years ago (really, I think she found me). She had been abandoned and given up for adoption several times in her little life. How anyone could not want that beautiful dog I will never know. When I met Basil, she was sad and lonely, afraid and depressed. She had lost the hair on her tail and didn't really trust anyone. Funny, sounds a lot like the girl I used to be.

But, with a little love and kindness and a place to call home Basil began to love again. She would roly-poly on the floor, and she loved chicken nuggets. She would come to sit by me for her morning love as I would pet her and tell her how much I loved her. Each time I would tell her how beautiful she was. And, in time, all of the hair on her tail grew back and she opened her heart to love again.

A few months ago, my sweet Basil girl passed on. How I miss her. Her unconditional love and gentleness have forever touched my heart. She just wanted to be with her Mamma. As I said my last goodbyes to her, I kissed her face and touched her fur one last time I told her, "You're so beautiful Basil, so beautiful." And, in that moment, I am sure I heard her say . . . "You are beautiful Mamma, You are beautiful." God did such a healing in my heart through that dog. Truly there is power in love.

And, by the way, as I am finishing this chapter God has blessed me with another sweet rescue dog. Her name is Snoops! She is so loving and kind. A happy-hearted girl who loves to explore—I think we are a perfect fit for each other.

Imagine God singing a song to you telling you HE thinks you're beautiful. HE does you know! He created you and designed you just the way you are. A unique, one of a kind masterpiece. You are HIS treasure! You are HIS jewel! You are the crowning glory of HIS creation! HE calls you altogether LOVELY, and HE delights in you!!! Receive that as HIS absolute TRUTH!!! You shall know the truth and the truth shall make you FREE!!!

**"What Would You Say" (Lisa Ritz. Copyright 2013)**

*What would you say in a song for a day if you knew*
*Would you dance in the wind~spin around~ laugh again if you knew*
*Perfect Love found you*
*Perfect Love made you*
*Perfect Love is setting you free*
*What would you say*
*So open your heart to His heart~let it just be*
*dance in the wind~ spin around ~ laugh again~dance in the wind~spin around ~laugh again~oh dance in the wind~ spin around~ laugh again*
*What would you say.*

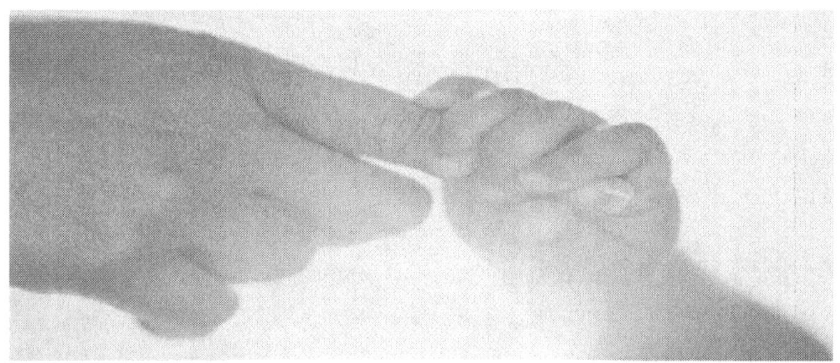

Papa God,

I thank you for these moments. I thank you for meeting me right where I was. I praise You for Your healing! Thank you, JESUS for rescuing me!!! It is YOUR finished work on the cross that saves, delivers and heals! Thank for making me feel like Miss America. Thank you for allowing my heart to know HONOR! And thank you for the day the tangible presence of your LOVE changed my world. And thank you, Lord, for singing to me…never has a sweeter song been heard!

Now, Father God, I pray that You hear the cry of every heart that reads these words. May You meet them right where they are. You know their hearts. You know exactly what they need. Papa, may they know the truth and depth of their beauty. For it is YOU who created them—a Divine Design. And Lord, may their hearts know HONOR! I release it in Jesus' name. God may each one encounter the tangible presence of YOUR love that makes all things new! And my sweet, sweet Jesus, may they hear You singing to them as only YOU can. Your voice singing to me was the sweetest song this heart ever heard. Now I release it over them.

In Jesus' Name I pray.
Amen.

Are there places in your life where you can feel that God is trying to heal your hurt? Have you felt rejection? Shame? Have you given up hope?

Ask the Lord to give you a song. Ask Him for the song that HE sings over you.
And wait. He will come. You may be driving down the road listening to the radio. Or you may be lying in your bed at night and the song of the Lord will come to you. It will bring you healing. I encourage you to write the name of that song here. Then write how that song made you feel.

Lisa
Kindergarten

Lisa
Senior

My brother, Brian,
my Sister, Kathy and Me

Auntie with the kids

My brother Brian and Me.
His Graduation

My sister, Kathy Rinard,
my Mom, Ruth, and Me

The Family Photo. Taken on our front porch at my Parent's home in May 2008.

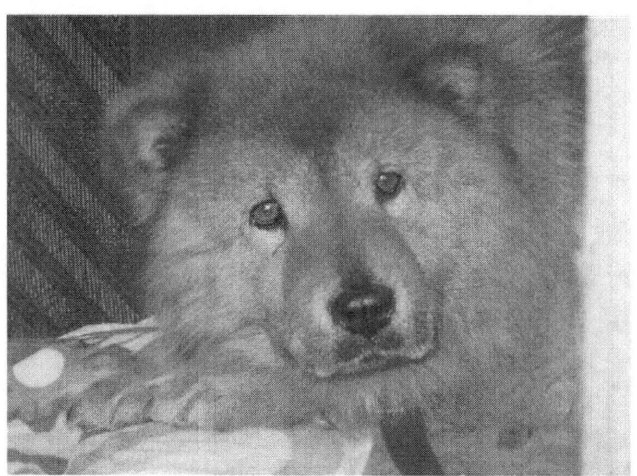

My Basil Girl….. my beautiful girl!

My parents anniversary.
Our last family picture in April 2007.

# Chapter Six

## His Lady

***"I am my Beloved's and He is mine"***
***~ Song of Solomon 6:3***

Where should I begin in this chapter? There is so much to say. So much I want to share with you. So much I want the world to know about the faithfulness of God. He is faithful!!! And HIS truth is greater than any lie of the world or any lie of the enemy.

Looking back, I realize that the attack on my life and on my little heart began at a very early age. The enemy came in and tried to steal my destiny . . . but he couldn't.

And though the years were hard, the path was difficult and the journey long…it is nothing compared to the love and faithfulness of my God.

In these next few paragraphs, I would like to paint a picture of the "me" I used to see and the real me HE created. Maybe you will see in my words the mistaken images you have of yourself and you will see the true beauty God has created on the inside and the outside of you.

I spent years trying to become "thin"—somehow thinking that was the answer to my pain. I tried diet after diet. Only to learn what I know my heart knew all along . . . diets don't work! They would only leave me feeling more rejected and ashamed than before I started. And somehow, I would manage to gain back even more weight than I'd lost.

There is a wonderful book about this written by Lisa Bevere, *You Are Not What You Weigh*. I have read it at least four times. A number on a scale does not define you and certainly is not the definition of beauty. You see, every assault that Satan sends our way is like an arrow. That arrow penetrates the depth of our soul, and it carries lies with it. Those wounds and the lies that come with them are designed to destroy and kill the real you. Some of those lies go very deep. And only GOD knows where they are and how to gently yet powerfully remove that lie and replace it with HIS truth. God longs to speak to us through intimacy with Him. He can speak to us through nature or songs, as well as through the Bible. I encourage you to make time each day to be alone with God. Ask Him to speak to you. You will hear His voice. You were

created to hear His voice and to know Him in a deep, personal way.

I remember as a little girl I dreaded things like gym class or going swimming. The thought of it would petrify me. I knew someone was going to laugh or snicker or say something cruel about my size. I remember the deep feeling of shame and embarrassment in those moments. And even at the young age of nine or ten, I believed no guy would ever want to date me. Not at my size. What was wrong with me? I felt hopeless and alone. Wow! There were so many lies the enemy told me . . . and that I believed. I hated my life at that time. Why did it have to be me?

Yet, even through those difficult times, I always felt the presence of God, and I took comfort in knowing HIM and being in HIS presence.

In my adult years, God began to deal with my heart. He challenged me to believe the truth about who I really was. I felt that somehow if my hair and makeup were perfect then no one would notice my weight. That belief had become an idol in my life. It was something I used in order to feel good about myself. It had come between my heart and the heart of God. One of the most freeing exercises I did was to go to a public place with no makeup and no hairdo. This was a huge for me. I begged God to let me out of that challenge. I think He must have chuckled, and so did I. I knew I needed to face the truth. I completed the exercise and it was very freeing. I still do it from time to time when I feel myself getting caught up in presentation.

Another challenge was to write down all the names I had been called through the years. There were names like "fatso", "tub of lard", "fatty fatty 2 X 4" . . . Lord have mercy those are awful things to say to anyone . . . let alone a child. As I wrote that list of names, I wept. Their sting was deep. I remember the laughter; the shame. I remembered how every day I was terrified to get on the school bus because I knew someone would laugh or say some cruel word. Then, once we got to school there was recess and the playground to give another opportunity for someone to make fun. Those years were filled with so much fear and pain. I faced it, one name at a time.

At the end of this exercise, God had me tear up the paper and declare those were all lies. Those words are certainly not what God says about me. Those were not the words He called me either. Then I had to ask the Lord, "What name do you call me?" "Who do you say that I am LORD?" And then came the healing—for it wasn't until I discovered His name for me that I could feel the healing inside of me.

All the words formerly spoken were gone. GOD stood up and called me "HIS LADY". I heard it so clearly. He still calls me "HIS LADY". That is who I am. And there is nothing that can ever change that.

Layer by layer, God began to heal my heart. He replaced the lies with His truth. He led me to places in HIS WORD just for me. And HE brought me friends to speak love and beauty. I learned that God's eyes are my mirror. His words about me are all that matter. This brought me such healing and peace.

It's not that the struggles don't try to come. It isn't that the enemy doesn't try to attack. It's that I have learned who I am in HIM. I have learned WHO made me. I have trusted in HIS WORD and HIS LOVE. I have taken the authority given to me by JESUS. I have learned to say the NAME, speak the WORD and plead the BLOOD! I have learned that I am HIS LADY.

He calls me altogether lovely. Beauty lies in the eyes of the beholder. The question is, who is your beholder? When you behold the One who gave His life for you, all else is lost. You become enthralled and captured by HIS gaze. Your heart knows the sound of HIS words and feels the sweetness of HIS touch.

There is power in the NAME of JESUS. He makes all things NEW!!!

In the next few paragraphs, I would like to share some of the intimate encounters I have had with my KING and some of the encounters HE has had with HIS LADY. It is my prayer that by sharing these next few moments of my life you will find hope and encouragement in knowing how deeply He loves us.

**My Deliverer**

Several years ago, the Lord began to speak to me about the early years of my life. There was a framed picture of me lying on the floor of my bedroom. I had planned to put it in a box for storage. One night as I was listening to worship CD, I

heard the Lord say "I want to talk to you about that little girl." At first, I was confused. I ignored the voice, but the next night I heard the same thing. I put the CD in and during a certain song the Lord would say "Put that picture up. I want to talk to you about that little girl."

So, I put the picture up, and I waited on the Lord. It was several days until I heard what He was saying/showing me. The song I had been listening to was about God delivering His people. It spoke of His faithfulness to rescue them. As that song would play, God began to show me a picture in the Spirit. I saw this little girl about four or five years old, and I knew it was me. I was very sad. I had been captured and carried away. I was riding in this old wooden wagon with tall spikes to keep me in. I noticed that the picture was black and white and the atmosphere was very sad. I kept looking back. When I looked back, the picture was full of color and laughter yet in that moment my world had turned sad, lonely and grey. I had been taken captive, and my whole life had changed. Deep feelings of sadness and chains of bondage engulfed me.

In this vision I was taken to a prison camp. The camp had grey stone mountains, and there were many other people in the camp. I felt so sad. I looked at the picture and wondered what happened to my life. What happened to the happy little girl with the great big smile? It seemed she was forever gone.

There is a part of that song where I could literally feel Jesus riding to me on a horse. And as He rides, He goes faster and faster. Ah yes, My Deliver is Coming . . . I could see Him in the distance, and then I realized He was coming for me. I

could tell He was riding hard and fast to get to me. He had fire in His eyes, and He was on a mission! He came riding into the camp, and as He came He reached down and picked me up and put me on the back of the horse with Him. Suddenly that black and white picture turned to color. As we rode joy began to bubble, and I knew He had rescued me. He rescued me . . . for My Deliverer had come. My joy had been restored! My life had been redeemed! I was FREE!!! I felt alive again. I felt the weight of the chains of bondage break off. I knew I had left that prison forever!

As we were riding, I kept looking back. I said "Jesus, there are still others in the camp."

He said "Yes, my child. You know how they got there. You know the way in . . . and now you know the way out." He told me, "I am sending you to the camp to set others free."

He will do the same for you, too! I don't know what prison camp the enemy has tried to keep you in, but I know the way out. HIS NAME IS JESUS!!!

He is faithful! He will rescue you! His love will allow nothing less! And when He comes and reaches out His hand, you must take hold!!! You must take hold!!! Be free my love!!! Be free!!!

**His Lady**

There is a song that speaks of being in the presence of the Lord that is very dear to me. I can feel Him inviting me to play that song and to come and dance with Him. It is as if He can hardly wait. I hear His voice calling me—His heart wooing me . . . Come Away My Beloved . . . Come Away . . .

So I get the CD, and I feel His heart leap . . . The music begins to play, and I see Him coming. It is my King, My Prince, and the Lover of my soul. Jesus—King Jesus—He is dressed in Royalty, and He is riding a white horse. Ah, seated in all His glory and splendor. And He is coming for me.

He gets close to me, He gets off the horse, He bows and says "Hello, My Lady." and I say "Hello, my King." He has the biggest smile on His face and perfect love for me radiates from the depth of His being. It is as if all sense of time and the thoughts of this world have vanished—for in this moment it is just the King and I.

After His greeting, He then asks me to dance. He takes my hand and we begin to dance together . . . just like a fairy tale. He takes His robe and places it over me, and He places a beautiful diamond crown on my head. Ah, the look in His eyes . . . perfect love. There is so much pure love when you look into the eyes of Jesus. It is as if His eyes were smiling. There is no fear, no shame, no rejection. We are fully accepted by Him.

The song has finished and the dance is over. He once again

bows and says "Thank you, My Lady."

I reply "Thank you my King."
He then says, "Until the next time, My Lady."

He gets back on His horse and begins to ride away, all the while watching me until we are no longer in sight.

My heart beats with excitement in His presence; I have never known a perfect love like this . . . only with my King. I miss Him already . . . and I have a funny feeling He misses me, too. How my heart longs for His presence. And I know He longs for me. He is my Royal Husband; My Heavenly Bridegroom and I ….yes I, am His Lady!

**"Come Away" (Lisa Ritz. Copyright 2013)**

*Come away, I hear the voice of My Beloved.*
*Come away I hear the voice of my King.*
*He is drawing me, calling me, wooing me, bidding me come.*
*Come away.*

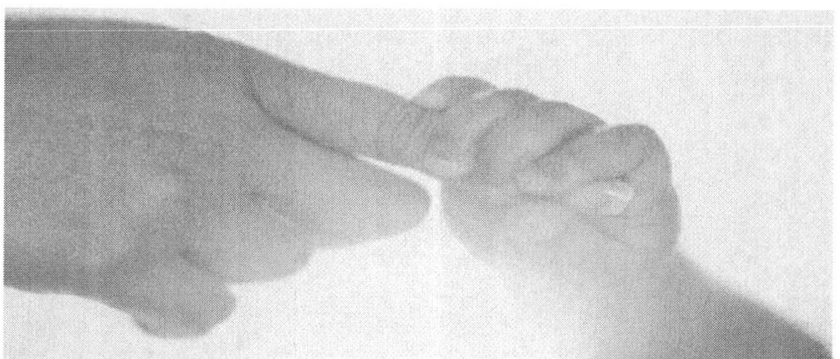

Heavenly Father,

I pray every heart that reads this chapter discovers who they are in YOU. It does not matter what others have said—only what YOU say about us is true. I thank you, LORD, that every negative word curse is broken in Jesus' Name.

I decree that YOUR WORD over them is faithful, powerful and true.

I thank you, Jesus, for the healing balm of Gilead! May it enter every deep wound of the soul and heal every part. I speak wholeness and life! And it shall be! It shall be!

And we give you all the GLORY—KING JESUS!!!

In Jesus' Name I pray.
Amen.

What words of hurt or negativity have been spoke to you or about you?

Now ask the LORD to show you what HE says about you?
Ask HIM who HE calls you?

## Chapter Seven

## The Song of the Heart

***"I will sing to the Lord. As long as I live I will sing praise to my God."***

***~ Psalms 104:33***

From an early age, I have loved music and singing. I remember the first song I sang was as a three year old. My Grandma had taught me the song, "Where the Roses Never Fade". I did not understand the entire concept of that song, yet something deep in my heart resonated within as we sang. Nothing fancy—just me, Grandma and Jesus in her kitchen. Though I didn't fully understand the meaning, somehow I knew I wanted to go to that place. I wanted to dwell in that land where the roses never fade.

Music touches places of our hearts like nothing else can. In fact, God himself loves our song. He dances over us and sings over us! That's amazes me!!! The Creator of the universe would sing over me!!! I wonder what His song would be? One of my early inspirations was my younger sister—Kathy. She went through our house singing all the time. She would sing songs about the Lord. With complete freedom she sang from a pure heart and with a beautiful voice. She would be so happy while singing those songs and it inspired me to let that song out!!!

My brother Brian loved to sing as well. We would turn the radio up loud and pretend we were the singers on the radio. We loved to sing together. Music has a way of bringing hearts together in a very powerful way. Of course, there was the time he put a bandana on his head and rocked out on his guitar to "Born in the USA". That makes me laugh 'til this day.

The radio was always on at our house. Country music was the genre. The motto was "If it ain't country…it ain't music." Country music at that time for us represented real life. The pure and sweet things. I have fond memories of those songs. They take me back home in my heart. They are places that will never be forgotten. They are also bridges to people who have since gone home to be with Lord.

My favorite class in my high school years was Chorus. It was near the end of my senior year that I met our new music teacher Dan Meredith. It was truly the hand of God. The Lord used Dan to believe in me enough to allow me sing a solo at my final spring choral concert. That had been my dream from

the time I was in kindergarten. Dan spent time teaching me melody lines and helping me with timing, etc. His encouragement opened doors for me when I was a very shy, insecure young lady with a passion and a dream to sing! He invited me to sing at his church and continued to encourage me through the years. Later on, that led to opportunities for summer concerts at a local park and outdoor sings on the back of a wagon. I have learned God will bring you the right people at the right time to help birth your dream.

In those early years, it was my music that kept me going. It was the music that stirred my heart and gave me hope. I listened to the radio for hours. God knew the desire of my heart, for it was Him that placed it there. HE guided my footsteps all along the way. As a young teenager, my hero was Barbara Mandrell, and surely I was country when country wasn't cool. Then, as I matured and became a much more serious Christian I began to listen to Amy Grant for hours. I love her voice and her sincerity. To me she was always just Amy. Her music and her words are honest and open.

I also always had a desire to play the piano. I took lessons for a few months during elementary school and always paid attention to the notes on the page when we were learning choral music. Many of my friends also sang and played the piano. I learned a lot just by observing them when we were hanging out in the music room or at the church in the evenings. Privately, I spent hours learning songs. I always had a desire to do more but was so afraid to play in public. Then one Wednesday evening at the Needmore Bible Church, Pastor Doug needed someone to play the piano. I was the only one

there who could play. I did not want to do it in my own flesh. I came up with every excuse you could think of to avoid playing . . . none of them worked. I told him "I can do it, but I can only play with one finger from the hymnal" (thinking that would stir him to let me off the hook). He said, "That is fine. That's all we need."

"You know," Pastor Doug said, "in life we tend to look at the nine fingers that *can't* instead of looking at the one finger that *can*", referring to my excuse for not wanting to play. I paused, letting it sink in. He continued, "If we would focus on the one finger that can—soon the one finger will become two and then three. The note becomes a chord; the chord becomes a song."

Those words changed my perspective on life. We just need to step out right where we are and trust God to lead us and grow us. He was right! That was almost 20 years ago and that one finger piano player now plays the song and leads people into the presence of God. Start where you are and let God grow you! He is faithful!

Time moved on and I began to travel around the U.S. I worked as a travel nurse for about seven years. God always led me to a church and gave me a church family. He always gave me at least one good Christian friend. I am amazed when I look back and see His hand on my life in that arena. I was blessed to sing under the most excellent directors. I learned something from each one of them. Sometimes I was only in an area for three months, yet by grace, I would be given the opportunity to serve in the music ministry.

I honestly cannot imagine my life without a song! Life is a song! It is the song of Heaven released into the atmosphere of the earth for such a time as this! In fact, the song of the heart isn't just music and notes. The song of the heart is the very essence of who we are and how we express ourselves. Each one of us is a song!!! Imagine your life as though it were a music box. It is full of treasure on the inside. We must open the lid to the music box to hear the song and see the dance of the ballerina girl. Perhaps you don't sing, but rather you are a writer or a sculpture. Whatever the dream is on the inside of you let it out!!!

This song in my heart was placed by my loving Creator, and it is one of power and majesty--yet at the same time it is gentle and tender. It is a beautiful expression of all that HE is and all that HE made me to be. We are not called to be like another. Each one of us is a unique, one-of-a-kind design!!! May I encourage you to trust the Designer!!! That thing that you feel makes you different is the very thing God placed in you to stand out! Shine!!!

The last decade of my life has been quite a journey. There have been many mountains to climb and valleys to traverse. Yet HE has been with me through it all. In fact, it has been during those times HE taught me the melody of life. The crescendos and the decrescendos directed by HIS hands and molded by HIS heart have created a landscape of learning and growth.

God continues to give me leaders and friends in Christ who allow me to sing this song GOD has given me. Thank you to

each and every one for believing in me enough to give me a chance to release the sound of heaven that is in my heart. And thank you, Lisa Koontz, for being my worshipping warrior and friend! I am forever grateful.

As I walk this road, my prayer is this . . . Lord God, may the story of my life be worship in your eyes . . . May the song of my heart bring you great joy. I am excited to see what the dance of this next "song" will be. To follow HIS lead and lean on HIS arm as we dance and sing and celebrate the gift of life. Truly, the song of the heart must be sung . . . it cannot be silent! Lift your voice—tap your toe—leap in the air and SING!!!

**"Sing" (Lisa Ritz. Copyright 2005)**

*Wonder of wonders*
*Lord of my life*
*Holy One*
*Ancient of Days*
*Alpha/Omega*
*Beginning and the End*
*Perfect in all of your ways*
*So I sing ~ I sing of Your love every morning*
*And I sing ~ I praise You with all of my heart*
*I offer to You this sacrifice of praise*
*I lift up my voice and SING.*

*The Song of the Heart*

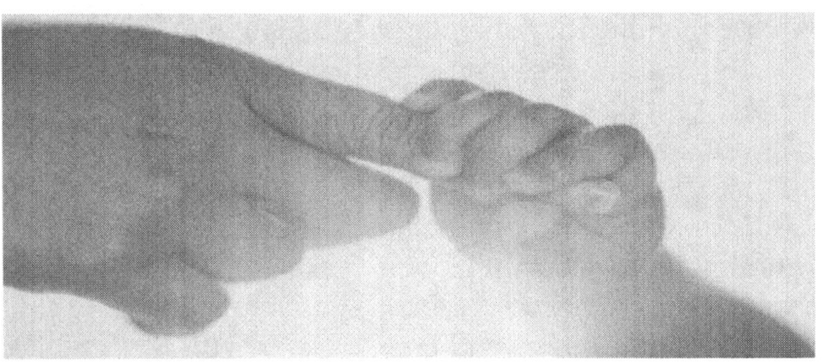

Heavenly Father,

I love you! Thank you for the song! It's your song Lord! You put this love in my heart! And I'll sing it to the mountain tops!!! You reign, King Jesus!

Thank you for all the folks you placed in my life to encourage me and teach me and believe in me.

Lord, I pray each person reading this book would find the song of their heart! Bring them the divine connections to help them along the way. And may they never ever, ever stop singing!!!

In Jesus' Name I pray.
Amen.

## *The Song of the Heart*

What is the song of your heart?

What brings joy to your soul?

~ Let the beauty of what you love be what you do!

# Chapter Eight

## Free to be Me

***"And she came up out of the dessert leaning on her Beloved."***
***~Song of Solomon 8:5***

There is so much in my heart that I cannot even begin to share. I am not sure there are human words to contain it. What is it, Lord, that You would have me say? What story would You have me tell? Do you ask God questions like this? Are you overwhelmed with the freedom He's poured into your life?

I am reminded of the story of Joshua and Jericho. I hear the instruction of the Lord: "Be strong and courageous"; "Go in and possess the land which I have given you"; "Shout for I

have given you the city." What is your Jericho? What is my Jericho?

Or perhaps we could talk about the life of King David! David was a shepherd boy that God made king. His journey was from the hillside to the palace. David knew both victory and defeat. Yet he lived for the Presence of the Almighty! This worshipping warrior ruled Israel with mercy and grace.

I think of Hannah and Samuel. This is one of my favorite stories in the Bible. For God needed a Hannah who would conceive and release a Samuel for service to the Lord. How the boy Samuel grew and lived in the temple and ministered to the LORD. I wonder what it was like for the boy child to hear the voice of the Lord?

And then, of course, there is the Book of Ruth. The widowed Moabite—a stranger in a strange land—who married her Boaz. He was strong, handsome and wealthy and of noble character—and because of Ruth's obedience and honor to the LORD, in an instant everything about her life changed!

I think of all of all these beautiful tapestries of the hand of God as I ponder the recent season of my life. This has been a process for me—a journey of the heart. And my Savior has been faithful to walk with me every step of the way.

I am grateful for the evening in October of 2011 that I went to Phil and Bernice Michael's home. The Lord had been peeling and healing me layer by layer. Now I wanted to move forward. I remember the love and peace I felt when I walked

into their home. How I loved the beautiful worship music and the banners.

We talked and prayed. Phil prayed and waved the banners and worshipped as Bernice led me step by step.

I took the authority given to me through Jesus' victory at Calvary. In His name and by HIS BLOOD and STRIPES, I claimed the victory that only HE can give.

I still feel the VICTORY!!!! There was a picture of Jesus on the wall and the song "Healer" played as we prayed. That night began a shift in my life that would lead to more breakthroughs in the upcoming year.

April of 2012, I began a life changing transformation process with Prophet Brian Kenney.

I had met Brian the previous year at a conference with Pastor Brian Lake. Normally I would never have engaged in conversation with Brian Kenney. Why? He is a Fitness expert and he is buff!!! (Don' worry, he knows about this—I have shared it with him several times) It amazes me how the Lord works. And yes, He does move in mysterious ways. This past winter I completed a weekend Boot camp with Brian! Hallelujah! (And I want a t-shirt!) This part of the journey is for the next book.

Layer by layer, we began to deal with things in my life. There was so much entanglement in the soul realm. There were sessions of the prophetic and times of warfare, as well as times

of just listening. Brian has proven to be an excellent mentor, coach and friend. He encourages me when I need it and guides me when I feel lost at times.
The transformation that has taken place and continues to take place is miraculous! I don't even recognize the person I used to be. The former years of pain and struggle had me in a state of fear, doubt, low self-esteem and intimidation. BUT GOD met me in the journey and HE delivered me! Beloved, I know HE will do the same for you.

I have crossed over Jordan and taken Jericho! I have journeyed from Moab to Bethlehem! I fought the lion; the bear and the donkey; I have slain the giant and cut off his head!!! Hallelujah!!! All in the Name of Jesus!!!

Beloved~ you become what you behold. I have learned to BEHOLD HIM!!! And, as I behold HIM, His eyes are my mirror . . . I see me . . . the real me . . . the one He created from eternity for this moment. I hear the voice of My Beloved, and I hear not the voice of another.

The ONE who created you defines you . . . defines me. It is in HIS PRESENCE we have our being. In HIS PRESENCE heaven and earth become one. He has called me away. My eyes have seen the Glory of the LORD and will never ever be the same. When you see HIM in all HIS GLORY and Majesty nothing else matters. When you hear HIS VOICE you cannot hear the voice of another. When you feel the touch of HIS HEART and HIS LOVE, every empty place is filled.

My search for love and beauty are fulfilled in HIM. I am

complete in HIM. And Freedom is a place of the heart. To be face to face and heart to heart with the very lover of my soul is perfect love! There will never be another who could love me like You, Jesus. This journey, LORD, has been worth it all! To know You in the secret place. To hear You call my name. To feel Your passion for me. To hear you call me YOUR LADY! I truly know I am free to be me!

I have been asking the LORD, "How do I carry the King? How do I carry such royalty and majesty—one of lowliness and humility? How do I carry the King? What would You have me do Lord? What would You have me say? To carry You to the nations! To release Your Glory! The ONE who is both the Lion and the Lamb. The ONE who is seated on the throne of Heaven yet rules and reigns in my heart. How do I carry the KING?"

So much you have done for me, KING JESUS!!! I give my life to YOU, Lamb of GOD. " Behold the handmaiden of the LORD. Be it unto me according to THY word," (Luke 1:38) I will carry You with gratefulness and gentleness, lowliness and meekness. Yet I will carry You with strength and power and majesty. I bow the knee to YOU—KING JESUS.

**"Love Would Not Leave Me There" (Lisa Ritz. Copyright 2013)**

*You heard my heart*
*You saw my tears*
*You felt my pain*

*You watched the years*
*~But you didn't leave me there~*
*Love could not leave me there*
*Love would not leave me there*
*~ I am redeemed~.*

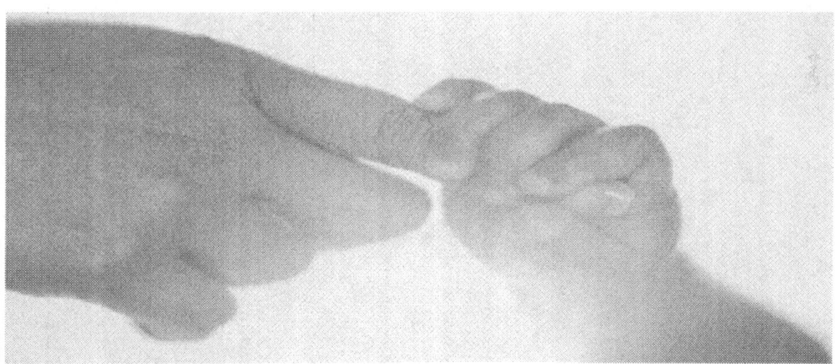

Papa God,

Thank you for your love and mercy. How you amaze me. I pray for each one who reads this chapter. May they find hope in YOU. May they know that the God of Joshua, David and Samuel is still GOD. YOU NEVER FAIL!!! YOU ARE FAITHFUL!!!

Meet each one right where they are, but don't leave them there. Bring them into the fullness of what You have for them. May they see themselves as YOU see them. May they look into YOUR eyes and gaze upon TRUE LOVE. May they know You more and more JESUS. And may they be forever changed

by Your presence.

In Jesus' Name I pray.
Amen.

God has a story for you to tell. What is it? What has He brought you through? What makes you different? They are all the ingredients for a miracle. List them below and ask the LORD what He would have you do with them.

My Grandma's and Me.
Gladys Ritz and Mary Shives. 1985

Mays Chapel Christian Church.
Warfordsburg, PA. (photo by Adrienne Ismail)

The Cowgirl!

My girl "Snoops" on
the day of her rescue

My Pastors
Brian and Pamela Lake

My Pastor Brian Lake and Family

My Coach ~ Brian Kenney and Me

Brian and Erika Kenney with Lisa

Adrienne and Auntie
(photo by Adrienne Ismail)

God is Faithful!

Thank you Lord!
(photo by Adrienne Ismail)

# Chapter Nine

# Thank You Lord

***"Lord who am I …. That you have brought me this far?"***
***~1 Chronicles 17:16***

Do you feel thankfulness? Do you begin to see the places He is whispering or shouting to you? Do you realize the greatness that is inside of you, given by the greatest power in the universe? I do. I feel His wonder and power. Where do I begin? How do I say thank you Lord? "ALL Thy works are wonderful. I know this fully well!" (Psalms 139:14)

I look back at the little girl with a big heart and an even bigger dream. The girl who wanted to conquer the Wild West. After all these years, I still see her. I still feel her heart and sense of

adventure. She is still fearless!!! She is more alive than ever before.

I think of the years I spent with my Grandma learning about the love of God. Watching the life of faith and love she lived and the Savior she loved. Father, I truly can say You do all things well. I didn't grow up in a musical family or a pastor's home. Yet I grew up in just the right place with just the right family. I am so very grateful. I would not change a thing.

I am reminded of the difficult years. The heartache and pain I knew as a very little girl, yet ***the sting is gone***....truly gone!!! I have been redeemed by the blood of the Lamb!!! I can honestly say it is well with my soul! My heart has been healed, and I have been set free!!!

The beautiful way you healed me, Lord. It was layer by layer. You are faithful. Only God knows the journey of the soul, and only God knows how to heal it. I remember the day I said "Yes" to You, Lord Jesus . . . ***I am my Beloved's and HE IS MINE!!!*** I will always love you!!!

The power of Your love is so amazing, so perfect!!! I am so very thankful for each person You chose to use in my healing. I am grateful for their love and kindness. How Big is God? Bigger than any heartache, any pain, any wound. I pray others will find the love I found in You—the healing I found in You. It is my earnest passion and prayer to take this love to the nations.

The encounters I have had with You, Jesus I will never forget. There is none like You! Nobody could ever love me like that. So deep, so high, so wide, so strong, so true. I have known You in a way I would never have known You. I have loved You and been loved by You in ways bigger than the sky and deeper than the ocean. How big is God!!!

Truly, I am FREE!!! Free to be me! Free to be the one I once thought was forever lost and completely ruined! The devil is a liar and the LORD reigns!!! I am ready to run this race You have set before me. I give my life to You, oh Lamb of God.

Papa God, so many times I would hear you say to me—

"Little Hadassah, Little Hadassah, Do you not know I have raised you to be a Queen?"; "Do you not know? Do you not see?"; "I have brought you to the kingdom for such a time as this."

You would say to me "Little Hadassah, do you not see your story is no different than that of the Story of Esther. For it is not so much about the fact the Esther was an orphan. It is the story of redemption. For I made her to be a Queen to redeem my people.

And the story of Hannah is not so much about the fact that Hannah was barren. Yet it was the cry of a pure heart who would conceive and release a little boy name Samuel—Samuel who would become a Prophet~ My voice to my people. See how the story of Ruth is not merely about a widow woman in a foreign land who needed a husband. It is the beautiful story of

the kinsman redeemer. How everything changed in a moment! And Ruth would have a son~ who would have a son~ who would have a son~ named David—the shepherd boy who became a king and of his lineage would come the King of Kings—Jesus.

The Lord would say to me, “Was I not faithful to them? And think not that I will not be faithful to you! For your story, Lisa, is not so much about the lost years of innocence or the painful words of childhood. Nor the lonely, lonely years of young adult life. And it is definitely not about your weight. See it for what it is. Look deeper. Go a little further. For it is the story of ***redemption***. A story of salvation, restoration and healing!”

“The little girl who longed to conquer the world—will conquer the world, in My Name,” says the Lord. “For you, my daughter, have asked for the nations and it shall be! It shall be! The years you sat at your Grandma’s feet learning to be an intercessor and a worshiper was handcrafted by ME. The pain that you experienced, the attack of the enemy was really an attack against me,” says the LORD, “and I am YOUR REDEEMER! I STAND for YOU my child! I am Your Deliverer!!! All the enemy has stolen he must give back seven fold!”

“I have taken the places of pain and shame and pulled out the lie of the enemy and I took the balm of Gilead and healed your wounds and even now I am restoring you to health,” declares the Lord (Jeremiah 30:17). “In all of this, you have learned the power of love and the song of your heart has been purified by

Holy fire—for you sing for me. Your song shall break chains and set the captive free! Your song rides on angels wings and you sing with the sound of Heaven. You are Free! You are Free," says the Lord!

"Now Go in My Name," says the Lord! "Heal the sick! Raise the dead! Cleanse the Leaper! Cast out demons in My Name (Matthew 10:8). For I have given you authority! Greater Glory! Greater Glory! Release my Fragrance to the Nations, for even as a little girl you have asked for the nations, and they belong to you! Love the orphan in my name! Speak forth my Word! Shine! Shine! Shine!"

. . . and I ask you Papa . . . How do I carry the King? How do I carry majesty and meekness? How do I carry royalty and humility? I will carry you in all your GLORY!!! Behold the handmaiden of the Lord! Be it unto me according to your word (Luke 1:38). For the power of the sword is in the surrender to the king.

"My daughter—each chapter of your life only brought you closer to Me," says the Lord, "And, really, it only made you love ME more and really, really—you wouldn't trade it if you could.

"I love you, Daughter! Princess Lisa! Rule and Reign in My Name! Truly, truly, you are ***Beautiful and Free!***

"Spread your wings, my Daughter, and . . .

***~FLY~"***

To God be all the Glory.

Amen.

**"Beautiful and Free" ( Lisa Ritz. Copyright 2013)**

*You rescue me*
*You run to me*
*You heal me with your love*
*You cover me*
*You care for me*
*Forever I am beautiful and free*
*Forever I am beautiful and free*
*Jesus made me beautiful and free*

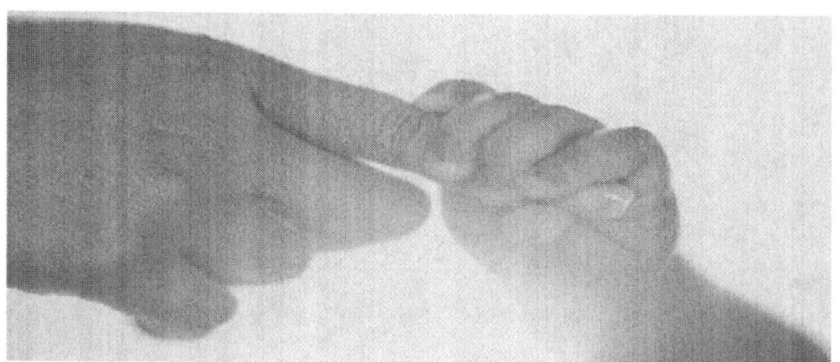

*Thank You Lord*

Father,

I pray each one who has read these pages finds true freedom and finds their true beauty in You! Thank you, Lord!

Take this moment to ask the Father to show you—you! And remember to dream big—all of heaven is dreaming big for you!

In Jesus' Name I pray.
Amen.

Personal Notes

## Lisa Ritz's Bio

Lisa Ritz is a passionate, surrendered lover of JESUS! She lives to worship the King of Kings.

Her greatest desire is to release the love of God to the nations through women's ministry, conferences, worship and missions. She longs to see people meet Jesus face to face and heart to heart—to be forever ever changed by HIS presence.

Lisa is an author, speaker, singer/song writer and prophetic worship leader with an anointing to bring people into the presence of God. She flows in the prophetic and has a strong compassion to bring wholeness to the body of Christ. Lisa's heart is to set the world ablaze with Glory Fire Revival, releasing the sound of Heaven into the atmosphere of the earth.

Currently she makes her home in Greencastle, PA.

## Lisa Ritz Ministries

### *Beautiful and Free*

Lisa Ritz Ministries is called to share the love of JESUS to the nations. Through women's ministry, conferences, worship and missions LRM is committed to seeing people know their true beauty and freedom in Christ. The heart of LRM is to fulfill the calling of Christ to love God and love each other (Matthew 22:37-39).